POWER PAMPHLET

Copyright © 2021 by Derrick Bliss

First Printing, 2021

Power Pamphlet

A Mindset Calibrator and a Practical Guide to Success

DERRICK BLISS

That's My Client

This one is dedicated to you.

"You don't have to be great to start, but you have to start to be great."
— Zig Ziglar

"I haven't failed. I've just found ten thousand ways that won't work."
— Thomas Edison

"Imagination is more important than knowledge."
— Albert Einstein

"Those who think they can and those who think they can't are both usually right."
— Confucius

"Happiness is when what you think, what you say, and what you do are in harmony."
— Mahatma Gandhi

The most effective way to do it, is to do it.
— Amelia Earhart

INTRO

Hey, just in case you don't make it past the intro, let me hit you with some important stuff right now. First off, don't stop at the intro - finish what you started. This is a pamphlet after all.

You can do this.

Second, for the sake of you and your well being and the unlocking of your power, please read as much as you possibly can in this life. It always blows my mind when people say, *I don't read*, when we have at our disposal, the vast collections of detailed glimpses into the minds of absolutely amazing thinkers, pioneers, philosophers, scientists, historians and dreamers. Yet some people just step over it all as they walk aimlessly through life.

The great minds of our planet have gone to great lengths to pour out all of their acquired knowledge on a topic, and to then distill and refine their words for you. Sometimes these works take years to perfect and only hours for the consumers to consume it, and yet still some choose not to read. I hope this pamphlet may stoke your flames of hunger for knowledge, if they need stoking. Please be hungry for more information and greater understanding. In fact, be ravenous.

There is a nearly endless amount to learn about almost any topic in the world of non-fiction and, even fiction, once you learn there is much truth about our past, present and future, buried in those beautiful lies. Knowledge is passed down through words and stories and pictures - we just need to remember to grab the baton.

And if we are missing anything in our great collection - some new ideas, theories, concepts, stories, topics never even thought of before now, please oh please, contribute. We need your help. Oh, and I beg you, please don't forget to let your imagination mingle with your knowledge, always and forever. Those crazy dreams of yesterday become the realities of tomorrow. Unless, of course, we dare not dream them.

Also, let's be real, some (not all) of you that claim not to read, spend a lot of time reading vapid posts about other people's lives on social media. If you just aren't into reading so many words in a book format, go with audiobooks. There are so many amazing works, both new and old, recorded and available in audiobook form. With audiobooks, someone literally reads to you while you drive to work, while you're on the elliptical or while you're laying in bed at night. How easy is that?

If you are interested in reading better and learning more, there is a fantastic book on re-learning how to learn, rewiring how you think and improving your reading skills, among other things. It's called *Limitless* by one of the great minds of our generation, Jim Kwik.

Part of power is greater understanding. As you open your mind and learn new things, not only do you have a greater perspective to aid you in your decision making and to put your mind at ease during seemingly catastrophic times, but you also start to comprehend that there is so much more you don't know, than you do.

When we only have a very small perspective, we tend to start believing that life consists of only what we see directly in front of us. I think of a young person taking their own life and it makes me incredibly sad because I feel so many would have gone on to live great and fulfilled lives if only they had a greater perspective. Also, think of the great contributions they may have made to this world or the positive influence they may have had on those close to them, causing a result of a more fulfilled life for them *and* those close to them, and therefore potential for even more great contributions to the world.

Since their perspective is limited to what they see and what they have seen to date in their lives, they feel that is it. They believe it is *everything*.

Their friendships or love life, or lack thereof, their clothes, their physical appearance, their mixed up and "crazy" feelings inside, what Suzie or Johnny thinks about them, the fact that they got deeply embarrassed over something at school or on social media - yes, all that can suck immensely at the time, but it's a blip.

When you're done with school and you learn more and see a little more of the world, you realize that stuff that felt like *everything*, was really nothing of great significance in your adult life. You also learn that if it was anything at all, it was an important building block for your growth.

Adversity is a key ingredient for growth. Most people who do great things and live great lives had to deal with adversity in one form or another, and that is likely no coincidence. It's dealing with these adversities that lead us down paths to build our knowledge and perspectives.

At some point, you will look back on your younger years and you may barely remember those catastrophic moments that felt like everything, and if you do remember, the details may be fuzzy because it wasn't important enough for your mind to hang onto. You might smile at the ridiculousness of how you felt and what you wholeheartedly believed to be true at the time, with your much smaller perspective. Or you may just be thankful for your life now and how it's so different from what came before.

If you are a young person reading this, I'm not giving you some abstract theory here, I'm giving you truth from a slightly greater perspective than what you have currently. If you are a little older, you already know what I am saying is true. Either way, I believe we now agree that growing your knowledge base and therefore growing our perspective, is wonderfully positive and fulfilling, so let us never stop doing that.

Please know I am writing this pamphlet humbly, as I recognize there is much more that I do not know about our power than what I do know. I believe our power goes vastly beyond what I can currently comprehend, and my intention is to continue to learn more and keep my mind as open as I possibly can.

This pamphlet was written to help put you on a path to unlock your power, to slightly calibrate your mind, and to bring your awareness a step closer to hyper awareness. I am sharing with you my thoughts and tactics for getting and staying in the right mindset as well as very specific, practical information about business that I have learned along the way. Some of it you may know and some of it you may not, as not all of us are exposed to the same information on our individual life paths.

So begins a journey to acquire more knowledge and grow, and this is a journey that is so rewarding that you will never want this journey to end. In turn, this causes you to be grateful for every day that this great journey continues for you, and gratitude is yet another part of power.

"Whatever the mind can conceive and believe, it can achieve."

– Napoleon Hill

"There is not a more powerful force than someone who has resolutely made up their mind."
- Derrick Bliss

power

1. The ability to do something or act in a particular way, especially as a faculty or quality.

2. The capacity or ability to direct or influence the behavior of others or the course of events.

My Idea of Power

Movies and books have distorted our view and association with the word power, making us conjure up an image of some maniacal villain with an unquenchable thirst for total control over others and domination.

It's not that.

Power is many things, all of which are personal. It's self control and discipline. Yes, control over one's self and the ability to be positive, to find success, and achieve peace of mind, is a form of true power.

But it's so much more....

1

You will fail.

The end.

Just kidding about the latter, but not the former. If you want to unlock your power and succeed in life, you have to be okay with failing. You don't have to like it, but you must understand it is part of the successful person's journey. It's as necessary as water is to the person on a journey through the desert. Drink in your failure. Learn from it. Sweat it out.

Now that all that is out of the way, let us establish, what is success? What is this thing called success you are striving for and why are you striving for it? Although I think success may be different for everyone, I believe it is always a byproduct or a result of one unlocking their power within. My best guess is that success is peace of mind. So, I suppose we will all reach the pinnacle of success when we drop dead, but if you can get to a really great place mentally, that seems to be success to me. Anyway, I'm also guessing you didn't pay your hard earned cash for this pamphlet to hear my philosophies on life and death so let's get to it.

Maybe you are a new salesperson ready to kick ass and take names or a veteran that needs a pick-me-up. Perhaps you are looking to change an aspect or aspects of your life. Maybe you are about to start a business or already have one, or you have other great ambitions or, you are in a doctor's office waiting room and this was the only thing laying around to read. No matter what - I want you to know that whether success is defined by you as financial freedom, more time to spend with loved ones, schedule flexibility, achievements, weight loss, living a healthy life, sobriety, recognition, respect, contentment, or some combination - it can be done. And I am happy to report that what you need to get there is already in your possession.

Have you ever run around frantically searching for your hat or your sunglasses only to have someone kindly point out that they are on your head? Well, that's what I am doing to you right now. Everything you need to succeed is right between your ears - past all that waxy gunk.

It's all in your head.

The only thing holding you back is fear.

Your mind can control you and your actions or you can control your mind. I'm not telling you it's easy. Most of us are hard-wired to stop in the face of rejection and to not even start for fear of rejection. It's scary out there. Trust me. I know. But you have to go out and get rejected. You have to be okay with failing. It does get easier. You do get more numb - your skin does get thicker - eventually you will have the epidermis of an alligator.

But yes, it's in your mind - the money you want to make, the flexibility, the recognition from others, the weight you want to lose, the respect you want to gain - all of that. First, you must decide (if you have not done so already) that you really want to succeed. Don't set a goal yet (unless you absolutely have to) but just resolve to be successful and to get, eventually, where you want to be. Try not to be obsessive and let this ambition destroy your quality of life or relationships, but don't let it leave the view of your mind's eye even if it is way off in the background at times.

Oh yeah, and the other thing I should mention is it won't happen overnight or over a week or a month or a year. It takes a long time and usually low earnings or miniscule results during that time - oh, and a potentially high stress level.

If it's successful entrepreneurship you're seeking, I should tell you that being an entrepreneur is like patrolling the ocean in a tiny boat with holes in it, alone. On this rickety boat, there is a big red button on the floor between your feet that says, "Instantly move to dry land. Work for someone else." (It has to be a big button to fit all of those words).

You can hit this button any time.

There are storms. It's scary. You are hungry. You are tired. You are under water at times. There are sharks in the water. You believe your success is out there somewhere and it is, but it's an ocean dammit. Finding what you're looking for can go on for years and usually does.

Most people hit the big red button.

When you see the ones who are successful, it's easy to think they got there overnight, but they didn't. They've been rowing their asses off.

Find me a success story that didn't start with multiple failures. Go ahead, I'll wait. Just kidding, I don't have time to wait. Now, conversely, go find me a failure story where the person never gave up and kept on growing and fighting. There is none. Because that is not a failure story. That story is underway, and has no ending. If that's you, here is your invitation to write your own happy ending. Or if you don't like the word ending, let's say happy lifestyle or just, happy life.

Power comes from empowerment, and all you need to be empowered is a slight mindset calibration. Once that's accomplished, anything is possible. And if business or monetary improvement is what you seek, this pamphlet will provide you with some concrete guidance and information to get you started.

When I talk about the mind and mindset, I think it's important to remember to mind your mind. Meaning, flip the inner light switch on. Be consciously aware of what your mind is telling you and if it is guiding you in the right direction, or if it needs a little adjustment. Being aware of your thoughts and never forgetting the power of thought and self-talk is the first major leap forward to having a key ingredient to power called self control.

A close relative of self control is discipline. Completing my books and getting my companies off the ground would never have happened with a total lack of discipline. Self control will make sure you are heading down the right road, and discipline is the fuel that you will need to get you from point A to point B. Awesome ideas die without the discipline to bring them to life. I find that sad. Please don't deprive the rest of us of your awesomeness.

Power and success starts and ends within. If you can agree with me right here and right now, that your thoughts are incredibly powerful, and that they will be a major factor in whether or not you find your true power, then we can continue. If you don't agree, I must politely ask that you reconsider your mindset before continuing. You HAVE to believe you can change, you can grow, you can adjust your thoughts, and erode the negative thoughts away over time - IF you work at it. Are you willing to do that work? Are you willing to start the heavy mental lifting or even the light mental stretching?

Making affirming statements about yourself is critically important. What you think and what you say is what you will become. So you can make either one of the two next statements knowing that we are all going to have issues and problems in our life.

Statement one:

My problems and issues will help shape me into something great.

Statement two:

My issues and problems will defeat me and I will never amount to anything great.

The choice is yours as to which statement you would like to say to yourself. But I'm asking that you say one or the other in your mind, and, out loud. Pick one and actually say it out loud right now, please. If you are on a train or in a place where you need to be quiet, then pick a statement and scream inside your head.

By the way, isn't it really cool and wondrous that you can actually yell inside your head and you can adjust the volume and the tone of a thought that's inside your own brain? It just goes to show you that the brain is super powerful beyond what we even know of its capabilities as of this moment.

Now, in both statements, you'll notice that we used the word great. Make me into something great or not great. I think it's important to point out that I believe the individual defines what greatness is in their own life. If greatness to you means being an excellent and happy toilet cleaner and living a nice life, then that's it. There is nothing but right about that. Personally, I would rather be a happy toilet cleaner than a miserable jerk with some fancy job.

When it comes to getting a hold of your mindset and making sure it's positive, getting started and forming the habit is the hardest part. It's like a thousand ton train just sitting on the tracks and we have to push it to get it moving, but once you're aware of what needs to be done and you do it, well, you pick up momentum and it goes all by itself. Maybe that's why they call it your train of thought. Probably not, but it ties my little analogy up nicely so humor me.

I'm not going to sit here and tell you that after you read this book, every aspect of your life is going to change completely, but I am going to tell you that if you take steps to change your life for the better, it will. I'm also not going to tell you that you need to start getting rid of all of the negative people in your life. Positive people can drive your motivation and so can negative people and sometimes we're surrounded by some really good people that are just more negative than we'd like and that's okay. In some cases it's more than okay and it helps to shape you into the person you want to be. So please don't go around thinking you have to get rid of everyone you know and become a totally different person.

However, I do believe you can either rub off on those around you, or those around you can rub off on you. If you are trying to change and better yourself and grow, but others seem resistant to that idea because they don't want you to grow or they don't want to grow themselves, make an assessment. You may have to do more internalizing your thoughts than externalizing. You may need to make some slight adjustments to your routine and schedule, but don't get mad about it. This is life. It's all part of the process.

You do need to develop your inner ninja. If one of your friends or family decided to throw a punch at you every time you brought up an idea for a business or a book or a movie or whatever it is you're passionate about, it would serve you well to learn how to duck or move out of the way of that right hook flying toward your face. The same is true when they throw an emotional, verbal punch at your psyche. Please just recognize that is what that is and then just dodge it, internally.

Meaning, don't let it derail you. If it annoys you, and proving them wrong is a motivator for you, then use it. If it stops you in your tracks and depresses you, just sway out of the way and keep it moving. But you have to dodge it. It may or may not be an intentional punch to the face, but it still stings. Even an accidental punch to the face hurts. So, just recognize it is what it is and reprogram the way you feel about that.

The bad news is that you will always have problems and issues to deal with, and you will always have some negative people in your life, but it is not what the outside world throws at you that defines you, it is how you deal with and react to what the outside world is throwing at you. You need to become a ninja when it comes to your emotional status. You need to be quick moving, nimble, stealthy and unable to be derailed on your mission.

Of course, there could be one hitch. That is, a negative party might reside inside your own head. Okay, let's not freak out, but let's work a little bit on getting a grip, a Kung Fu ninja grip, on our self-talk and our self thoughts. That is to say - our thoughts about ourselves, and our ability.

When we start talking about sales later, some of you might immediately say, "Oh no, I can't sell."

I need your inner ninja to whack the snot out of that thought. I don't really care if it's a karate chop or a 360 roundhouse kick, or a straight punch to the nuts of that kind of thought, but we need to get rid of thoughts like that. "I can't" or "Oh, not me" or "Oh, I could never" seem innocent enough, but if left to their devices, can destroy everything.

Again, it's okay. Everyone has thoughts like that to overcome. We will work up enough strength and quickness that we will be able to dodge these bullets with ninja stealth and zen calm, over time. And the nice thing is you don't have to move a physical muscle to accomplish this.

It happens between your two ears. That is where *everything* happens.

When I say everything, what I mean is, everything. You want to lose weight, it's about mindset, you want to start a business, it's about mindset, you want to make 10 million dollars? It's a mindset. You don't care about money and you just want to live a happy, broke life? You guessed it. It's about mindset. You want to become a martial arts expert, it's about mindset.

In an overt attempt to belabor the point because it's that important - I certainly don't want to be so vague as to just say change your thinking, but I do want to say you have to make up your mind first. And you might have some long standing desire to do something, but that is much different than making up your mind to do it.

As you're reading this, can you now see that minor but absolutely major difference between the two? Do you see the vast expanse between making up your mind to do that thing, and just having some desire to do that thing?

I have some long-standing desires yet to be accomplished. If I'm being honest and I don't want to be dishonest in life or in writing, I can tell you that the ones that are still yet to be accomplished are the ones that I have not definitively, wholeheartedly decided that I was going to do. They are desires, and they are real, and they are strong, but yet I have not made that monumental leap.

Like the major jump that Neo in The Matrix has to perform, this leap happens or could happen without even so much as blinking my eyes. It will happen all between the seven inches or so of my two ears. Yep, and it still has not happened. So what does that tell me? First and foremost it tells me that it's really up to me. It's not up to any motivator, it's not up to any life coach, it's not up to any guru or boss or mentor or family member or friend or business partner or anybody - it is up to *me*.

Your success with whatever that is, money, happiness, sobriety, weight loss, traveling more, developing a certain skill, all of the above or something entirely different, is up to *you*. When you decide that you are going to do something, when you resolutely make up your mind, is when it will start to happen.

So, what the hell will magically happen? Nothing will happen magically.

This is not a magic pamphlet.

2

Next, you will need just two little letters from the modern English alphabet, d & o - do. You will need to show up. You are going to have to do a lot of those things you don't want to do. Go to that meeting. Be at that function. Walk into that group and introduce yourself. Most people don't do the things that need to be done and don't get to their destination.

But, again, don't do anything until you've decided wholeheartedly that you are going to go for whatever it is you've been longing to go for. Do not waste your valuable time if you have not decided that. Don't waste my time in explaining all these things to you if you have not made that decision. If that's the case, the first step I would recommend for you is put this book down or stop listening to the audio version, and think. Turn off all your electronics and just think.

We can start the thought process by first asking, what do you really want?

What do you want for your next year, your next five years, your next ten years?

Write it down even if it's outlandish. But you have to remember, this is what you want, *not* what you have decided to take action on. Identifying what you want is a monumental first step, but remember, it is a huge, groundbreaking, earth shattering, worlds-apart difference from making the decision to do and doing.

Of the things you're thinking or writing, what is the first one you are going to decide that you are going to accomplish or conquer? If they all seem too out of reach or too impossible, it's ninja time. That internal ninja of yours has been waiting to kick the ever-loving daylights out of all those ideas about how you just can't do it. Close your eyes, picture that ninja doing what it was born to do and crane kicking those negative thoughts right in the chin.

My inner ninja's strongest throat punch in defense against the negative thoughts is positive thoughts. It sounds simple, but it takes some calibration to first even recognize that there is an attack happening that needs to be defended against, and second, to be prepared to defend.

An issue for me at times is fixation on certain negative issues or potential outcomes. The clandestine attack from within, lulls me by making sure I firmly believe that the issue or potential issue is something I *should* be fixated on. I have to train my brain to notice it and start to focus my fixation on positive things.

Yes, I may have to deal with a pressing issue, but there is a difference between dealing with something and being fully consumed by it. So I focus on the many things I am grateful for, and remind myself that there will be better days. Sometimes it's extremely difficult when you are in the middle of a storm, surrounded by dark clouds, to see that there are the most beautiful sunny skies just up ahead.

So, those positives can help me. Maybe a long walk or a massage or hitting the gym works for you, but one way or another that inner ninja needs to do its job so that no one gets hurt, especially you.

A helpful hint for you, after all you did buy this pamphlet, so I should probably start to give you some good stuff here - start to develop some very, very, very simple steps towards your goal. And to make it even easier for you, start to develop just one super simple step, a SSS if you like acronyms. Develop one little action you can take.

You want to write a novel so one step may be to write a chapter, but that may not be a super simple step for you. A super simple step may be opening up your writing device of choice and writing one word. If you're feeling good, write down one more. The action taken, regardless of the size, is empowering. Your inner ninja has won this battle.

Be happy with these tiny movements of progress. Remember, this is going to take time. Stay the course. Find joy in your small wins.

Everytime you made one sales call when you didn't feel like it, put down that extra spoon of ice cream, didn't take that sip, walked away from trouble, got on that workout machine when you were tired, you were tapping into your power. More than likely, it felt good. You were taking action. You were *doing*.

The decision started in the mind. It then manifested into a real world action. It would have been easy to give in to that inner voice that advised you otherwise, but your mindset grabbed hold of the leash.

I am pointing this out because it's important that we recognize and understand what happened in those examples described. They probably seemed like no big deal, inconsequential, but they are not. When a strong voice inside demanded that you eat that extra scoop of ice cream and you put the spoon down anyway, you powered up. We need to realize that an interaction, or more to the point, an inner confrontation, just occurred in that moment.

See, if you don't realize that is what is happening in your mind every day, then you are floating around, easily yanked in this direction or that, for better or for worse. Awareness is one of the keys to unlock your power.

Would you join me for a little more off-roading about mindset before we move on to the next section? If you came across a genie in a bottle that could grant you one wish, what would it be? Well, guess what, you have a genie in a bottle. The genie is your brain and the bottle is your skull and it has the power to make some of your biggest wishes come true.

It's funny to me that many people will exhaust all of their internal power and energy to find material things in the exterior world, when we could use the internal power we have, to bring those things to us.

I think of buried treasure. I love the idea of hunting for buried treasure as much as the next person, but the reality, and the irony, is that we all have buried treasure within ourselves that most of us don't even want to explore or pay any attention at all, yet we are excited to go hunting for someone else's treasure.

So let's recap what we've learned so far - you will fail, you'll take emotional punches, and your own thoughts will work against you.

Surprised? You shouldn't be. The vast majority of people do not reach the level of success, which they pined for, abstractly. Or, they went for it and it didn't work and they tried again and then they stopped. I believe it's out there for anyone who wants to go get it, but how long it takes and how great it is, varies from individual to individual. The constant thread, that must be woven through all those tough times, is your unflappable belief in yourself and continuing to be conscious of, and working to improve on, your mindset.

Ninja, do your worst.

3

Once we know what we are dealing with, we can start to combat it. The mental enemy is a part of you. It's part of your brain. It is not vindictive, rather innocently pragmatic, in its quest to fulfill its purpose of getting what it wants right now. It is only doing its job, but that does not mean it is not the opposing force that is working against you.

So, if I can liken that part of your brain to an adorable little animal that appears to be innocent, then you might see that it is possible that your brain, a cute little puppy in my case, can be swayed in this direction or that, but it is not being malicious. Your mind can be easily manipulated into doing things that are ultimately not good for you. Your mind is so powerful that suggestions or ideas of harmful activity most times are expertly camouflaged as something enjoyable and no big deal. The consequences, both short and long term, are pushed way off into the background.

This is a part of your own mind working against you, at times directly counter to your hopes and aspirations. Why does your mind do this? I am not a doctor, but I believe mostly all of us are wired with basic desires which can provide fuel necessary for survival. Maybe we just have to do a better job of deciphering the good ones from the not so good ones. I do think that just being aware of this is a great start. Not every idea served up by that part of your mind is a winner.

Your thoughts, your inner animal, can control you or you can control your thoughts. If you were offered drugs at an early age and accepted - the drugs themselves were likely not the reason that you took - it was your inner animal's curiosity, or it was your desire to be accepted by the group, to fit in, for your inner puppy to be petted, in other words. It's hard to deny an innocent animal something that it wants, but if it's bad for it, well, you need to be aware of that and identify that is what it is, and you need to be strong because it's bad for you.

If you're addicted to drugs or battling addiction of any kind - your inner animal is in control and simply does not know what's bad for you, what is wrecking you, what is keeping you from your true power.

Puppies will eat chocolate and get very ill and throw up and go to the bathroom all over your house, but that chocolate tasted good so in spite of all that, the same puppy will go and eat chocolate again. People do the same things to themselves. It's hard. Our inner animals are persuasive, so much so that we don't even know we are being persuaded. We have to be awake and we have to fight.

My inner puppy is incredibly convincing and sweet, but that son of a bitch (we're talking puppies so I can say that) will drag me down a detrimental road daily, into oncoming traffic, if I give in to its demands.

Now, since what we want is results, I don't yell and scream at my puppy, I don't smack my puppy, I'm not mean to my puppy and I would never tell my puppy it's no good.

This will only cause my puppy to shut down and might even lead to worse behavior then what it was doing prior. Also, I don't want to lose the innocence of the puppy because that's the part that dreams and one needs to be able to dream to achieve one's dreams.

If you think the innocence of your inner animal is lost forever, you're wrong. It's in there. We need to rediscover it to unlock its true potential. Then we need to protect it by building up our inner ninja.

So how do we nurture our inner innocence while also protecting it from doing harm to itself? Well, you just took a huge first step - just being aware of what this is and how it will negatively affect your vision for yourself. You need to associate those things that are not good for you and things that will work against you, as exactly that. Whether you make a mental list or written list, or just weigh each thing out as it comes your way, this heightened awareness will help to insulate you from those poor outcomes.

You need to reinforce this, just the way you would reinforce puppy training. You may even reward yourself for doing the right things and deprive yourself of awards if you make the wrong decision. Whatever works for you.

I will now belabor the point as I think it's that important. Apologies in advance. There is a part of all of our brains, call it your inner puppy, or whatever you like best, that works against us. I am calling it an inner puppy because, again, I think it's innocent and not malicious in any way. By making that comparison, I am understanding of it. I will need calm resolve and patience to win this battle. My inner ninja moves in silence and deploys wise strategy and tactics to accomplish its mission. The less emotional your inner ninja gets about doing its job, the better.

That part of my brain, the puppy part, simply wants to satisfy some need, to fulfill some urge, and that is its function. Just like anything else, once I learn it and recognize it when it's happening, I am more equipped to handle it.

I am not going to get mad or angry at it as I simply know it's time to power up my vision. My vision is one of the weapons wielded by my inner ninja. We'll get into your vision shortly, but basically it's what I'm working towards, it is the destination of the path on which I am travelling. But my inner puppy is so cute and enthusiastically yanking me down another path - the path of, 'ahh, forget your inner ninja', the path of, 'just relax', the path of, 'don't make those sales calls', the path of, 'just eat that extra ice cream', 'take that drug', 'drink that alcohol', etc.

It can be so damn persuasive - I know. I am not trying to oversimplify anything. I've been in the clutches of addiction, I've seen it take down people extremely close to me, I've also seen many sales people fail from the jump, or start out strong and then fail, and I've seen countless diets that did not stick. Your vision, the life you are driving toward, is like your inner ninja's sword and so it must be sharpened, and it must be used to protect you if you want to unlock your power.

This battle is fought and either won, or lost, inside your mind. Try to remember, this will not seem like a battle when presented to you. It will seem as innocent as a puppy - oh, come on, it's just this or just that - and you may find yourself making a little deal because the animal is so cute and persuasive. You might find yourself thinking something like, eh, okay, I'll just have the one or take this break from it all for a little while or whatever, and that's it.

I'm not saying don't have fun or celebrate victories, or if it's a diet, not saying don't have your cheat days, but please oh please, don't get complacent. The minute you get complacent and lower your level of awareness of the potential pitfalls, is when your inner puppy will go to town on that chocolate.

Lastly, if your life is being affected by someone else's addiction, please try to keep in mind that the addicted person's inner animal is being controlled by a strong force. So, if you have to be mad, be mad at that force - whether it's drugs or alcohol or any addictive behavior. Don't be mad at the person. They are us. We are them. We can all be susceptible to this type of force. Please remember, we are dealing with an issue within the mind and so that is where the work needs to happen to correct the issue. I know it's hard, but don't give up. Just like we are all susceptible to addictive behavior, I believe we all possess the tools to overcome the addiction. Some of us are not afforded the time to locate those tools and overcome.

My hope is for you and your loved ones still with us, you will discover the necessary tools and practice using them. Just like cutting back tiny branches in front of you in a dense jungle, the minor adjustments made within will start to reveal a new path. Keep going - little by little, branch by branch, until you find your way.

4

Mindset and thoughts, good or bad, are muscles you build and are trained behaviors. You have to make a conscious decision to put in the time and constantly work at getting your mindset to the proper place.

Over some short time, like riding a bike or driving a car, you will get to a point where you require much less conscious thought to operate in this positive mindset. Do you remember when you first started driving? You sat in the car, had to remember to put the key in the ignition, turn the key a certain way, check your mirrors, remind yourself which is the brake and which is the gas, hands at ten and two, don't forget the directionals, which one is a left turn signal and which one is a right turn signal, how to put the car into reverse, drive, neutral, what to do when you're backing up, and on and on.

Not too long after doing that process constantly and routinely, you found that you started to do many of those things without much conscious thought or effort. It's a trained behavior. You were taught the basics and then trained yourself so well that you can now do them without even thinking about it. Look at what a good self trainer you are without even realizing it.

Of course, the example of that thing you now do without much or even any thought, may not be driving, but my guess is you won't have to look too far to find a similar example.

Disclaimer: this is not a driver training manual. Perhaps consult your local driving school if you're interested in learning more on that topic. :)

Oh, and one more thing - by unlocking your inner power, you will be helping others. You may be doing this consciously and on purpose by building a great company or from your philanthropy or in a number of different ways, or you may be doing it unknowingly just by the mere fact that you are unlocking your inner power. You have no idea how inspirational this can be to other people. Some may tell you about it while many may never tell you about it, but people watch. People see that you can do it and they feel empowered. That alone might start them on their path to unlocking their power.

So try to remember to not be so selfish. Try to be more selfless. Yes, this pamphlet is for you, but helping yourself *and* helping others will also further help and fuel you. This is part of unlocking your power. You are not just unlocking your inner power for *you*, you're doing it for a bunch of other people, for all of us.

5

Okay, let's get into some business stuff, but I would like to point out that the business stuff is also, of course, mind and psychology related. Remember that people buy things and do business with you or your company mostly based on emotions, AKA how you make them feel. Keep that in mind as you formulate your next steps. People also make decisions about whether or not to start or continue a relationship with you based on how you make them feel - exhausting right?

The good news is that it's one of those things that, generally speaking, the more you put in, the more you get back. Put effort into invoking a positive experience with your customer and personal relationships and watch what happens. If it's all about you, you, you then it will be you, you, you losing all power. So, am I saying that you ultimately have to give power, and empower others, to unlock your power? As of now, based on my life experiences to date, I would say yes.

Focus on the good experiences you want for your customers and loved ones, uplift those around you as best you can and watch what happens. And a tip to get you started on your uplifting journey - one of the simplest things you can do to create a good experience and uplift those around you is show gratitude. Have you ever been to a fast food restaurant, or any establishment for that matter, and the person behind the counter took your money and then said nothing. They missed an opportunity to say sincerely, "Thank you for your business," and more importantly, missed an opportunity to make you have a better experience.

Don't miss an opportunity to say thank you. Be thankful and show it. Even as a customer or just as a person in everyday life, we can say a sincere thank you too and it feels good for both parties. It's a powerful thing.

Don't be maudlin or over the top about it, but be genuinely appreciative of both the little things and the big things, and the universe will return in kind.

6

I'd like to now offer you some practical advice that may help you on a path to financial success.

You may have no money or very little and no rich uncle or aunt. Then again, you may be filthy rich. Congrats!

In this next part, I want to give you some of my thoughts and ideas about getting started in business.

So, maybe you do have a rich relative, but they are frugal, or you don't want to get your family wrapped up in your business dealings. I get that. Okay, but you need some startup capital, right? More than likely you do. If you believe in your idea and/or your plan, then you might borrow money - assuming you *can* borrow and assuming it is with reasonable terms. If this is not an option, or, if you just don't like that option, I'll suggest another one.

By the way, I would like to point out that we are now embarking on a key brick in the building of your success and the harnessing of your inner power - which is exploring multiple options, inside and out, not settling until you ventured into each nook and cranny of potential outcomes from different paths - in business and life in general. In other words, asking yourself, what's the immediate effect of this decision? What are the possible issues this may cause down the road versus the possible advantages down the road?

Try to really think these things through. Don't be immobilized by overthinking as it is important to try new things out, but don't be so cavalier either. Even minor missteps can ripple into big problems and usually some upfront conceptualization can help guide your decision making.

Even if it doesn't work out, it will be a learning lesson, maybe a minor or major setback, but don't let it stop you. We make the best decisions we can with the information we have at the time. Do remember though, you have a world of information available to you in the form of an online search engine.

Back to the loan. If you borrow money, you have to pay it back. You see? Now we're really cooking, huh? But yes, you have to pay back the money, and more than likely, with interest. And you *do* want to pay your bills on-time and straight away - building a good rapport and trusted status with vendors and lenders will prove invaluable down the road.

Another thing to consider is you likely have to start making those loan repayments just about immediately. So you want to be relatively confident in your timeline of when you start generating revenue to pay the loan. What you don't have to do with a loan (in most scenarios) is give up a piece of your company. This might be important to you now and may be more important to you later, or not.

You could run into a scenario whereby a non-bank, meaning a private investor may give you extremely favorable terms on a loan, but in exchange requires a separate Warrant Purchase Agreement or Warrant Exercise Agreement. Having a warrant agreement in place gives the holder, likely this investor person, the right to buy shares or a percentage of the company at a certain price before the expiration date noted in the agreement.

A reason why you might consider doing something like this, is that the terms of their loan may be much more favorable than a financial institution or online lender. You also may not be able to get approved in those places. So, you turn to a potential private investor, or ideally more than one, and either one of them approaches you with this idea or you bring it to the table to try to get a deal done or to get yourself more favorable loan terms.

A reason why the investor would do this is they are getting their loan repaid, likely with interest, and they have the option to buy a piece of your company at a fixed, predetermined valuation. If the company takes off to the moon during the time period of the warrant agreement, the investor exercises his or her warrants and purchases stock in your company, probably at a below market valuation in this scenario. They likely just have to give you back your principal payments you've made to that date.

If the company is just knocking around, not really growing, or worse, not doing well, they can let their warrants expire and there is no obligation for them to buy a piece of the company. So, it's a somewhat low risk position with potentially big upside for the investor.

Again, think these scenarios through carefully. Assuming the business does great, as is likely your plan, do you want that person as a percentage partner in your company? Maybe yes, maybe no. How much percent, if any, would you be okay with them owning? Think, think, think.

If you decide to attempt to borrow money personally, pay close attention to your debt to income ratio because your potential lender will likely be looking at that. Debt to income ratio is how much you earn monthly compared to what you must pay monthly and how much debt you are currently responsible for repaying. This may be tough for you if you don't have a lot of income right now.

For me, I put borrowing personally in the last resort column as there are many ways to get creative. Everyone operates differently.

Please do your research beyond this pamphlet. This is important stuff. Consult a lawyer, accountant, or other people you trust, and then make the decision you feel is best for you and your goals.

You may have guessed about another option to get the start-up cash you need - sell a piece of you or your company. There's a million different ways to structure a deal with someone, but one simple way can be to tell someone about your vision and plan and the opportunity and see if they want a piece of this on the ground floor.

The risk to them is, of course, that it crashes and burns like many new ventures, but the upside may be great if they give you a chance. Depending on your arrangement, they may get a minority equity stake in your company - maybe they own ten or twenty percent and maybe they have say-so in the company direction and maybe they don't. Everything can and should be outlined in an agreement of some sort.

Ownership and employment are two different things. Some people own part or all of a business and also work there and get a paycheck. Some people own part or all of a company and do not work there and do not get a paycheck.

Maybe the owner will just receive a percentage of the overall profit when the company decides to issue profits. These types of details and more should all be outlined in an Operating Agreement so that everyone is on the same page.

Keep in mind - unless the investor shares the same vision as you, you probably want their help with the financing only and you may want their advice from time to time, but that may be about it.

A potential investor will likely be interested in your vision, financial projections, and a marketing plan.

Depending on what you're doing, intellectual property may be important. Having a patent on a process or product can be incredibly valuable to the business, and to potential investors, and can also help to protect you against lawsuits.

Disclaimer: I am not a lawyer and cannot provide any legal advice. I'm just providing you with some information as I understand it, based on some research and my experiences.

Prior to 2013, the U.S. had a first-to-invent stance on determining who was the rightful owner of an invention, but the laws have changed. Now, the policy is that the first-to-file a patent application is the rightful owner.

To find out if there is an existing patent issued for a product similar or identical as the one you have in mind, you can hire a patent lawyer to perform an exhaustive search. Depending on the results, you may opt to proceed with your own patent application or decide to go in a different direction.

If you're curious, you can do some keyword searches on your own as well. Google has a search engine dedicated to patents called Google Patents.

The reason why it can be important to know if a patent exists (if you think you may be preparing to sell something brand new and unique) is that you don't want to start mass producing and selling something only to find out you are infringing on someone else's patent. That person may opt to take legal action against you. This type of situation would be double bad.

You may also want to look into a trademark. Maybe you want to trademark your business name, or your business logo, or a particular product or service. Within the U.S., you can apply for a trademark with the USPTO (U.S. Patent and Trademark Office). They have several different product and service categories, so you would choose one or more that would best fit your business type.

I have secured a patent and a few trademarks and I usually work with a good attorney whom I trust. My friendly suggestion is that you do this as well.

7

Now, let's think a little more. After all, it's thinking and it's the mind that will get us to where we want to go. Let's think more about finances and what are the reasons we may need money. Is it primarily going to be used for personnel? If you are in a highly service-oriented type of business, personnel may be critically important to the success of the venture. If that's the case, you may not need much of any money if you are open to being creative.

What you have is a company, a business - or you soon will. You might find that the best employee you could hope to bring on board to help build your company, wants to be a part of your company. Maybe there is a potential partnership opportunity worth exploring.

Great - but be careful - proceed with caution! You don't always know how a partner will be in six months or a year or three years, especially if things are not going well. This zero cash approach can end up being quite costly down the road, but you might decide to take that risk because you're broke right now.

Try to make the best deal with as many potential scenarios as you can reasonably predict, entering into your agreement. Ask as many "what if" questions as you can conjure. It's hard because you are working with the limited knowledge that you have now and likely, without a crystal ball. If you have a couple of bucks or a family friend that practices business law, get a consultation and brush up on potential scenarios and pitfalls to try to minimize your exposure.

It's important that you thoroughly think about partnerships beforehand, no doubt. Definitely don't throw caution completely to the wind and go into an incredibly important arrangement like that, haphazardly. Partnerships can be game changers in a good way and also in a pulling-out-your-hair way.

Two pieces of advice I can share that may help you on your journey - one, good communication is key to making most relationships work, and two, nothing is set in stone. Although it may feel like things are iron clad because of a contract in place and that may be the case right now, but things can usually be worked out down the road if both parties are willing to talk. New contracts can be drafted if there is a meeting of the minds.

Now, let's say the business becomes successful, starts taking on new shape and growing new tentacles and the original partnership just doesn't work anymore for any number of reasons. The best scenario for all involved may be for you to buy out a partner or, if you are the partner that no longer wants to be a part of the company, try to work out your own buyout. In business and in life, things change, evolve, grow and shrink, so try to work on your pliability. Be firm with your principle beliefs, but be flexible enough to be open to new and different situations. If you're not stretchy, you can't grow.

The other thing you can do with no money and no willingness to bring on partners or give up a piece of anything, is find people to work on a percentage. This could be a commission or just some sort of splitting of proceeds. Some people are willing to work on commission like this for some time - especially if it can be lucrative for them. Of course, make sure that it can be lucrative for you too.

Weigh out if you want to pay a little more to them now because you need to grow a following of steady clients - maybe you do and maybe you don't. Keep in mind, the accounts in the long run will likely be more valuable to you as it's your company. You are growing your equity, the value of the company you own, as you grow that book of business.

Paying based on margin, opposed to paying on the total sale price, provides structure and autonomy because your team will clearly understand the business, how it makes money and directly connected to that, is how they make money.

What the heck is paying based on margin?

In other words, instead of paying a percentage of the amount of the total sale price that is made, paying a percentage of the margin of the sale that is made. The margin being the difference between what it is sold for, and what it costs, all-in, to fulfill it. For example, if you sell burgers for $5 and your all-in cost is $1.50, your margin is $3.50. So instead of paying commission on the $5, you pay it on the $3.50. Each one of your items will have a different margin and your empowered sales person will know the fulfillment cost of each one.

But won't everyone at the company will know all about your business? Yes. This will start to create a culture of leadership as everyone starts to feel a shared responsibility and takes ownership of the company. This is now more than a standard j-o-b.

Compensation dictates behavior - how you pay will determine the outcome and hopefully, the desired results. If you want to drive certain behavior, make sure that your comp plan is structured to drive that behavior. And think about long term behavior, not just short term. Right now, you may have an insatiable appetite for new, new, new business, so you may have an urge to have comp very heavy on new and less so on existing clients. Proceed with caution because in one year or ten or one hundred, you want your existing clients to be treated just as well as your new customers coming on board for the first time.

Also, when I said "all-in" cost when talking about margin, be sure to consider all costs associated with that burger - the ingredients, the wrappers, the napkins, the sauce, the cost of the employee's wages that rang it up and prepared it, etc. Every business will have different costs inherent with making and fulfilling a sale. Keep those top of mind when creating the comp plan best for your business model.

The theme with all of these scenarios is use your mind power. One thing you always have, whether or not you have money in the bank, is your ability to think and be creative. You want to buy a million dollar business, but don't have money and the bank will not lend you any?

Get creative.

If the business is worth it and you can pay the owner back in monthly payments and with interest over several years, the owner might seriously entertain it if they are looking to make an exit. Also, in this scenario, the owner is acting as the seller and the bank, so *they* are the ones collecting the principal payments *and* the interest.

Most people are more open minded to a well thought out plan than you may think. If they are motivated, and they trust in you to deliver, it has the potential to work out well for everyone.

Lastly, remember the currency you always have at your disposal, even when you're flat broke, and don't underestimate its value - kindness. Just being kind and respectful to people can result in them sticking with you in tough times, giving your product or service a try, or happily partnering with you to help carry out your vision and the bonus - being kind is just the right thing to do. Basic? Yes, but overlooked by some would-be successful entrepreneurs.

8

In my opinion, the top people are the ones you should pursue and try to retain to help you build long term. If you have a chance at bringing these types of people on board, do what it takes. Make the best deal you can, but get the best people and treat them well. It's the people that will make the difference in your project. Don't blow it before it starts by cheaping out, but don't give away too much either and demoralize yourself. Try to find a happy middle ground while remembering - no one will work quite as hard as you, no one will bear the burden quite as great as you and no one will care as much as you.

Okay, so assuming it's business success you are after, you've taken a huge step in deciding that you are going to start the journey. Remember though - deciding is not doing. The first step in the journey is deciding, but the next step is just as critically important - and that is, taking the very first outer action. It can be small, but it has to happen to start the momentum.

But what should it be? You ask. Well, it's good that you're asking a question. Your first outer action will likely be the answer to one of the following questions:

Am I starting a service type business or a retail type?

I like service businesses because services are always needed and they can be close to free (depending on the service) to provide. People and companies will inevitably need services of different sorts and the more you grow your business the more people you can employ which helps the overall economy.

Can you start a service business without being an expert in that particular service?

The answer is yes. The secret I am going to give to you right now. This is a secret that many successful business owners already know. It starts with another question.

Are there successful businesses where the employees are more skilled at the services and more expert than the ownership themselves?

Again, the answer is yes. The secret is simply that she or he who starts the business, has a business. Meaning, if you can figure out a way to get some customers and connect them with the service people, you have a business. You will need some sort of system to manage your customers and staff, but it doesn't have to be a complex system. Some of the most expert and skilled people in certain areas lack the simple way to get clientele or develop an easy management system, or maybe just don't want to be bothered with getting the clientele.

To me, a business is selling anything that makes people's life easier. That could be a product or a service.

So, how do you become a business? You form a corporation - maybe a C-corp, S-Corp, LLC or another type. You can do this online, or just consult with an accountant. Many business owners have an incorporated business for one company and another incorporated business for themself as they themselves are a business as well. Your self business may ultimately end up involved in multiple ventures and will incur expenses related to the involvement of all those ventures, and some of those expenses can be business expenses.

Again, I am not a CPA or qualified to give any tax or investment advice. Consult an accountant with specific questions about business accounting.

One of the businesses I am in is digital marketing services for businesses. Our clients can spend their valuable time learning the services we provide, and then training a team to work on them, and manage that marketing team, pay the payroll, etc. etc. Or, they can make their lives and businesses run smoothly and focus on their growth by hiring our team at a much more reasonable cost of time and money.

Me and my team took care of all office cleaning for a short while, but as we became busier and busier, it became apparent that our time was more valued on our digital marketing activities, so we hired and paid an office cleaning company - a service business. We can certainly do what they are doing, but it makes us more productive and makes the business operate more smoothly with the help of their services.

Other questions you may ask:

How will I get my first customer?

Maybe it's a post on social media, maybe it's a group text to your friends, maybe it's making a few calls, handing out flyers, pinning your business card at the local car wash etc. Maybe this is not your first step, but at some point soon, you will need to ask this question. To help with this question, you may want to ask a different question first, *who* is my customer? Meaning, who is my ideal customer? The answer will help you identify the best strategy to reach them.

How will I accept payment?

If you want to take credit cards, you will need to establish a business bank account. In order to establish a business bank account, you will likely need an EIN, an employment identification number. You will get this once you're incorporated. Do some research on incorporating and what type of entity will be best for you and your business. Again, there are some online sites you can go to for incorporating, or talk to an accountant. They can usually help you with the process. It ranges from a few hundred to a few thousand dollars, depending on the entity type you set up.

How will I keep track of my customers and projects and/or billing?

We use Quickbooks, Google Drive sheets, and some other programs. The good news is that you are living in an age where there are so many great computer programs to help manage your business that you can utilize by simply paying a small monthly fee. Punch a few phrases into your favorite search engine and check it out.

How will I get people on board to work for me?

If you don't have anyone in mind right now, you can reach out to friends and family to see if they know anyone that fits the description of a good candidate for you. Or, you can post on social media, or you can pay to post it on an online classifieds site or a job/careers website.

My philosophy is that regardless of experience and education, a person is likely going to have to learn much of how your company will operate and your process, from the ground up. Therefore, I look for someone that seems to be bright, enthusiastic, open to learning new things, and overall will most likely fit within the culture of the company that I am trying to build. Ultimately, I want someone on board that wants to be there, wants to be a part of what I am doing, a self starter with leadership qualities.

The last thing I ever want to do is have to look over anyone's shoulders. Once someone is trained, I am there for support as needed, not babysitting.

How will I pay my employees?

You can do this manually, work with an accountant or work with a paycheck assistance company such as ADP, Paychex or others out there. Personally, I work with a paycheck assistance company because for me it's easier and gives me peace of mind that it's done properly and timely, and I'd rather invest my time in other areas.

What are the first steps at a minimum I need to take to even get started? Maybe a business plan or a business card? Maybe a website or social media page, maybe creating a bill head or an invoice?

How will I make sales?

9

We are about to start getting into some sales. Hey, Reader's Inner Ninja, please be alert here.

You have to sell. Period. End of story.

"But I'm not a sales person. I could never sell anything. Wah wah wah."

Stop whining. You sell all the time. You just don't realize you're doing it. Remember when you said, "But I'm not a sales person. I could never sell anything," just before? Assuming you said that or some variation then you were attempting to sell me on the fact that you're not a salesperson and more to the point, you were trying to sell yourself on that "fact". Sorry, I'm not buying. Hey! Your first rejection. That wasn't so bad, right?

More on the danger and irony of saying you can't sell, in just a second. First, I'd like to point out that you sell all the time. I want pizza - but *you* want Chinese food. I want to go here - but *you* want to go there. And on and on. You sell all the time. I want pizza - but *you* want Chinese food. I want to go here - but *you* want to go there. And on and on.

Do you have a favorite movie or tv show? Can you tell me about it enthusiastically? When you're passionate about something, it's natural. It's not forced at all. You need to find something you believe in.

Sales is just getting someone to see things the way you see them in your head. If your reasoning makes sense to you, it's just a matter of explaining it properly to someone else - finding the best way to connect it to their receptors, their way of thinking.

If you can order a double chai super spicy chocolate latte with skim milk and whip cream, you're ready. Oh, and if they forget the whip cream, and you can politely point that out and persuade them to add a little bit on there for you, you are more than ready. I know the reason you can do that is because drinking that delicious latte is important to you, but so is your future.

Okay, but you're shy and don't think you could talk to people. I can easily prove that's not true. Watch what happens when we go out knocking on doors or partner up on some meetings, if I ask you *not* to talk. Please don't say *anything*. You will find that not only do you have something intelligent to add to the conversation, but you also can't wait to throw it in.

The danger and the irony of the statement, "I'm not a salesperson."

The danger is, of course, as Henry Ford once said, "Whether you think you can or you think you can't, you're right." The mind is an incredibly powerful thing and when you condition your mind by telling it you are bad at something or you just can't do something, what will happen is you will in turn become bad or just won't do something.

The inverse is correct as well. If you change your statement of, "I am not a salesperson to instead say, "I am a heck of a salesperson," watch how your life can change. Watch how you'll be more receptive and open to the many opportunities that exist around you. You need people to be involved if you are going to find any level of success.

The absolute irony of the statement, "I'm not a salesperson," is astounding. Because by telling yourself that statement and those around you, what are you doing? You are *selling* yourself and those around you on the fact that you are not a salesperson. And if you do it enough times, and say it with enough conviction, guess what you are going to succeed at selling yourself and those around you? Yup, you've sold that you are not a salesperson so congratulations, you are a heck of a salesperson.

I had some serious doubts about whether or not I could sell anything as well. I was always more on the quiet side, especially around new people. Speaking up was challenging. I got anxious when it was my turn to order my sandwich at the deli counter. Those around me were surprised when I told them I was starting a sales position.

What I did have was a firm belief in the company and its product, and I had a burning desire which gave me the necessary drive. I wanted to do it and prove it to myself, but also, I wanted to build out a new path that I felt might lead somewhere great. I worked with amazing and experienced people and I became a sponge, learning everything they would teach me.

I was still quiet. I chose my words carefully. I chose to listen as much as possible and to just try to make real connections with open minded people.

I dealt with a lot of rejection just like anyone else. Not everyone is open minded right now, but I found that they might be tomorrow. Also, I learned that some of the most open minded people can give you the toughest rejections out of the gate. This is the security wall they've installed in front of all new ideas to protect them from making a poor decision. Unfortunately, it might prevent them from making good ones too. Sometimes it's hard to know the difference.

When you're met with a harsh rejection right away, it pays to say something like, "No problem. Just out of curiosity though, did you have a bad experience with (whatever it is you are offering)?"

They might open up a little, or they might say, "None of your business. Beat it!" Either way, you'll be fine.

If your tone is right and you approach them humbly and curiously, you have a good chance of getting a good reception. Don't worry about being a talker, concentrate on your tone. You don't have to say much at all. Just say things in a tone that lets them know you're not a threat and your intentions are good.

The real truth is it takes more discipline to listen more than you talk. Refraining from talking, especially at the right moments, is important and also a learned skill. In other words, when it comes to sales, don't worry about talking, worry about not listening enough. Focus on listening. The best salespeople are the best listeners. Go out there with a goal of seeing how little you can say in your conversations with prospects and clients. It is better for you anyhow. You want them to talk more and they want to be heard, so, respectfully, please shut up.

It's a common misconception about being a good salesperson that you need to be a talker, or pushy or smooth or maybe even a loudmouth. The good news is you need none of those things. In fact you only need two things - belief, both in yourself and in your product, and drive. The rest will work itself out.

"The rest" may be other important aspects like being organized, the words you'll need to say to sell the thing, the courage to say them, the bigger courage not to say anything when you're supposed to be listening (and *really* listen) and so on and so on. All of that will be there if you believe in the thing you're selling and believe in yourself and you have made up your mind that you will succeed.

Oh, and always have basic good manners of course.

Do NOT try to be something you're not. You have a mousy personality? Then that's who you are. People buy honesty in the most beautiful and uglier forms. Be honest. Tell them the bad news! But maybe they won't buy if you're that honest? Some won't. BFD. More people will ultimately buy than won't if you are honest and you are truthful about the good and also about the not so good about what you're offering.

Now I would like to both take the pressure off of you and increase your sales performance at the same time. I do this by reminding you of the truth - sales is not about you, it is about them. Why put pressure on yourself to sell, when to sell effectively, you need to focus on your client or prospective client. The quote from Theodore Roosevelt, "People don't care about how much you know until they know how much you care," is absolutely true.

How do you show how much you care? Stop selling! Phew. You see? No more pressure. So, what do you do? You make sure you focus on the most important step of the sale - probing, or, asking questions. The best salespeople understand that it is about the needs of their clients. How can you know the needs of your clients if you are busy blabbing on and on. Ask questions and focus on the answers. Write the answers down even. Show them that you care. Again, be sincere.

A simple formula to help you on your journey is as follows:

Sincere + Bold = Sold

So, if the sincere part comes from just being real, asking questions and keeping the focus on them, what about the bold part? I've found that most people like to buy, or invest in something, especially with someone they like. Unfortunately, most people probably don't feel comfortable shouting, "I'd like to buy now!" in the middle or even at the end of your conversation. This is where you being a professional and being a little bit bold, will make the difference.

Bold can come in the form of asking a closing question, or in the form of an action such as just proceeding with the paperwork at a certain point. If you are proceeding straight to the close, you can qualify that they're ready by asking a basic question as you are entering their info such as, "What's your zip code?" If they give it to you, you're on your way. If they say, "Oh, wait a sec. I'm not sure I'm ready to do anything," well, you can just let them know that most move forward and you feel strongly that it's good for them, but just ask them what's up. We need to know what they are thinking. What is the issue?

They will likely give you a reason they can't do it now. If the reason is that someone else is involved in the decision making, then we need to work on better qualifying the appointment beforehand by seeing who gets involved in making this type of decision. Not the end of the world. Maybe you can set up an appointment to come back and talk to all parties involved with the decision making.

If it's a different objection, just talk about it. Maybe they aren't sure if it will work for them. Let them know that's totally understandable. Perhaps review the benefits a bit more. Inform them that most people feel that way initially. Remind them that the only way to truly know how great it is, is to try it. Remind them about the minimum commitment, the entry level, etc.

Another way to be bold and go for the close is just asking a closing question like, "The big package is amazing because you get all of that, but most people feel comfortable coming aboard with this middle package. That's the most popular. Which one do you think is better for you?"

Which one is an either or question, opposed to a yes or no question. Your job as a pro is to make it easy for them to buy because you know it's good for them (assuming of course, that it's good for them). Don't deprive them of what you have and the benefits of it, by forcing them to shout, "I'd like to buy now!"

Some personal thoughts on finding your power and success in sales. Do your best not to let it be your only success and your only business. Many of us want to rack up the zeros on that balance sheet or in the checking account, but while I have your attention, let's talk about the real scoreboard.

There's 8,760 hours in a year and you're sleeping for somewhere around 30% of those. The older you get, the faster a year zips by. You blink. It's over.

Don't lose sight of the zeros that matter most. How are your numbers of laughs with your kids or your friends or your nieces or nephews, mom, dad? Focus on getting those numbers up too, with those that are still here with us.

Make sure you exceed your hug quotas and you smash your goal on listening intently to those in your life and being there when they need you.

I've lost people close to me way, way, way sooner than I ever would have imagined and the only thing left in the giant gaping holes drilled in my heart, is perspective.

Don't *try* to find a balance between your professional ambitions and your loved ones. Find the balance dammit. Sleep less. Do what you have to do. Get it done.

Unlock your power, fulfill your potential, but find the balance.

Do you know how many of us will look back at the end of our life and regret enjoying it, or regret spending quality time with loved ones?

Zero.

10

Now, this is by no means a diet book, but let's talk about weight loss. Although, I have tried several different ways of losing weight over the years and I will share with you what has worked best for me.

First off, as is the common theme in this pamphlet, you guessed it, losing weight absolutely starts within your mind. The power over your mind or control of your mind is what will undoubtedly make the difference in your weight loss effort. I know this to be true because I have lived it. To be more specific, I saw a documentary that put into light what many food companies out there are trying to do to get us to eat more of their products regardless if they are good for us or not.

They want us to eat more and if their product is addictive, then even better for them as more sales will be made. In other words, everything is stacked against you out there on your journey to lose weight. It was this knowledge, and the subsequent adjustment to my thoughts about and toward certain food types, that enlightened me and led to my losing over thirty pounds over the six months that followed my watching the documentary.

It changed my perception of certain foods, and illuminated the game I was a part of that I didn't even know was being played by some companies.

I lost those thirty plus pounds after watching the documentary because it was so eye opening, and what I really mean to say is - *mind* opening. Before that, I gained the unnecessary thirty pounds because my mind was being trained by outside forces without me even being aware of it. My inner puppy dog was chasing after every hoagie and ice cream truck it saw and I was not equipped with the commands to stop my puppy from that behavior.

It's important to note though - the companies are not the enemy. The enemy really resides between your ears. Once you know what is good for you and bad for you, the only enemy is your own mind.

Once I flipped the switch mentally and saw things through the lens of my newly found knowledge, it was easy, or at least, easier. The bullets coming at me slowed down - prior to that, I didn't even realize anyone was shooting at me. During that time of losing those thirty pounds, I did not visit the gym even one time, so I learned another valuable lesson - weight loss is mostly about your diet. If your goal is losing weight, you have to change your diet - period.

Of course, exercise is good for you, so whether you go to the gym or not, it's a good idea to maintain some kind of exercise regiment. But don't go crushing it at the gym everyday and don't make any change to your diet, and expect great results. Making that change to your diet, starts with the change in your mind. And when you flip that switch, remember that your inner, adorable little animal, can be easily lured over to that tub of ice cream - which is perfectly okay - sometimes.

Always, always, always remember - please - this part of your brain will come calling at some point - maybe late at night - you have to first be aware that a part of your mind is now betraying you, and you must bat it down - day in and day out. The good news, if you can do this at night, then the next morning, the other part of your mind will be thrilled - that puppy will be wagging its tail and happy to see you.

So what works best for me is something like carb cycling. Everyone's a little different, but a very low sugar and low carb plan is what helps me lose weight. What I found though, is that when I would do this strictly for long periods of time, my body started to feel like it was lacking. Also, I wouldn't get to eat some of my favorite things, like, forever.

I heard about carb cycling from watching a video by Vince from V Shred and the concept made sense. I may not be doing it exactly right, but what I am doing is working for me..

The basic idea, as I understand it, is that if you don't eat any carbs or sugar for an extended period of time, your leptin levels, fat burning hormones start to diminish and then even your digestion can slow down. So by spiking your carbs once a week or so, you avoid this from happening. What I do is, every sixth or seventh day, I go crazy on whatever I want - pasta, hoagies, ice cream etc. Then the next day I'm back to a low carb, low sugar intake, and I'm eating foods I truly enjoy, but those foods without the carbs and the sugar. I lost a bunch of weight, feel stronger, and I always have something to look forward to each week. Win win if you ask me.

Disclaimer: I am absolutely not a dietician or a physician or physical trainer, just a person that has tried some different diets over the years and found one that I like best.

P.S. If you start out strong and are doing really well with your life change, whether it's a new diet or quitting smoking - again, at some point your mind may turn on you and encourage you to go ahead and eat this or that or just have that one cigarette or whatever behavior it is that you're trying to change. Stay the course. The results will be worth it. Be strong.

11

Special as a Dog

I love dogs and I think they are amazing creatures. Therefore I was excited about the idea of comparing myself to a dog. We've discussed mindset and the importance of it, but let's make sure that you believe it can precipitate change for you and not just for me and anyone else other than you.

Consciously starting when I was in sales for someone else's organization and especially when I decided to go into business for myself, the most valuable and important thing (maybe the only thing) I had going for me is my mentality.

"I am going to make it. I'm going to build a successful business in one shape or form or another."

It was something like these thoughts inside me, nestled firmly in place - even on the terrible days. Maybe it wasn't even that specific, but it was an underlying belief. I just would keep going no matter what comes my way. There have been so many failures, but really temporary defeats, along the way, and it was that underlying belief that always got me back on course.

That is the main reason why I have found some level of success to date which brings me to my point. When I talk to people about this, their mindset and the negative part of their brain usually reacts first by saying something like, "Yeah but that's you. You're different. You're special."

For me, I'm as special as a dog. Meaning my mentality wasn't always this way. Your mindset, good, bad or indifferent, is a trained behavior. If you see a dog that can sit, jump up, rollover, or give you it's paw on command, do you think, *Well, the reason this is possible is because that particular dog is just special. Other dogs can't do that.* My guess is you probably say wow, that dog has really been trained well.

My guess about this dog's success is that it took constant reminders and reinforcement and many little steps along the way, to end up with the finished product - a dog doing cool things on command. The dog probably got distracted many times and went off course, but the good trainer kept working at it, nudging them back on course. Was it a perfect journey? Absolutely not, but we don't see that journey here. We see a dog performing well.

Others will not see much of your journey either, especially because much of it takes place inside your mind, but they will see the results eventually. You have to remember as often as is possible, that you are both the dog and the trainer. Your journey will be imperfect and you will get distracted and pulled off course temporarily. It's okay. It happens to everyone. Just make sure your belief and resolve is nestled firmly in place and you will get back on track and one day, you'll be rolling over and getting that treat.

Now, if you tell me that some dogs out there will require less training and get there faster than other dogs, you will get no argument from me. For some dogs, it may take longer and there may be a few additional steps, maybe some different tactics deployed, but if you really work at it with the dog, they can get to the behavior that you're seeking. The same is true with people and their thoughts, and their thought process.

So, am I special? Yes. I'm as special as a dog, and almost as smart as one. I know. Stop bragging, right?

12

INFA Mentality

I'm not f****** around.

Or, I'm not fooling around. This simply means you turned the knob on your mindset to, "I'm on a mission" status. You're in the right mindset and you won't be driven off the route.

You'll have minor setbacks, you'll have times of insecurity, you'll have times of doubt, and although they might slow you down slightly, they will not stop you from your mission. Because you're not f****** around.

I am absolutely not suggesting to develop an angry or bitter or mean exterior. Rather, I'm saying that you need to be resolved and resolute about your definite purpose.

Nobody even needs to know about your mission of unlocking your inner power, except for you. In fact, I don't think we should tell anyone just yet. We will flip the switch and we will move about our work, taking very small steps on a big and rewarding journey.

But, even though you may not tell anyone about this change, there will likely be an outside perception of it from others and this perception will start to alter the way people react to *you*. It's a shift in your energy and as a result, the universe, the world around us, will shift in kind. Just don't take this lightly. That's all I ask.

INFA means that you are taking this seriously. And seriously doesn't mean for a day, a week or a month. INFA is you being committed to the long haul and if you can't do that, oh, well I'm afraid to report that you *are* f****** around. Revisit this when you can get serious. And when you can commit. Because it's at that time, once you cross over that threshold, that magical things may start happening.

Did you ever come across someone that has firmly made up their mind to accomplish something? You can tell that nothing and no one can make them change their mind?

That is powerful.

13

Don't be a host.

I believe the vast majority of people are good, but there are some bad ones, and there are good ones who are in a bad place, temporarily. Some of these people want nothing more than to pull you down to their current mental state and have you join in their misery.

These people are toxic and extremely contagious. You can be dragged down to their level and ruin your life just as easily as catching a virus. The minute you give in, you become the host to this virus.

Let me give you an example. You're driving down the road in the slow lane, listening to a Derrick Bliss audiobook, enjoying your day. Some guy starts aggressively riding your bumper. Then he swings into the left lane to pass you. He scowls at you while passing and then gives you the finger. This person is in a bad place right now. They are the virus and they're looking for a host. If you take the bait, you're the host.

What if you get mad, curse at them, cut them off? Meet up later at a red light, fight them, go to jail, or worse, they shoot you. Was it worth it? Of course not.

You became host to a terrible virus and you didn't even realize it. It's easy not to realize. It's easy for your emotions and pride to cloud your judgement. It's more difficult to take a deep breath and just stay in your lane. Take the deep breath, let it go. Otherwise you may deprive yourself and all of us of your true power. And for what? To become a statistic? One more road rage incident.

Here's another - you're walking along, minding your business and someone is standing against the wall, eyeing you up and down as you walk past. This other person shakes their head at the sight of you. Then they make a sound like, "pshh," indicating they think very little of the sight of you. They are a virus, doing everything in their power to find a host. They want *you* to say, "What are you looking at?" and then, you're it.

Just keep walking, faster if you need to. Heck, run if you have to. Don't engage. Let them talk smack in your wake. Let them rant and rave.

Don't be the host.

You have a lot of good to do and likely, so does that virus, once they get to a better place mentally. Don't judge them. We've all been in a bad place at one time or another, but don't be the host.

Choose peace over pride.

Of course, there are some situations that demand intervention from us, but most do not. There are many more virus/host situations out there so please be aware. Some are in your face while some may be more subtle. Be conscious. Be present. Have self control. You'll be happy you did.

I think certain music and media can be responsible for activating viruses from the inside of people, more and more today. This results in more viruses, yes, but also more people who may be susceptible to being a host.

We've talked about how powerful your thoughts are, so therefore be protective over what you allow to permeate and occupy space in your mind. Musical lyrics can easily become your mantra. With the wrong mantra, meaning listening and repeating the wrong type of lyrics, your mentality can shift out of focus, and your whole personna can change. I've seen it, firsthand. Don't sleep on how powerful music can be. Choose what you allow to enter and occupy your mind, carefully and wisely.

Maybe the stuff you like listening to has an amazing beat, intoxicating even, but lyrics that are no good for you. This is junk food for your mind. If you really love it, think of it like ice cream (assuming you love ice cream like me). If you eat ice cream all day every day, your body would be unhealthy, you would likely gain lots of weight and end up with medical issues.

If you're listening and watching the junk food for your mind, you are doing mental damage to yourself. You are actually getting in the way of nurturing the gifts you have inside, getting in the way of reaching your full potential and unlocking your inner power.

Please don't shrug this off. Music is your mantra - food for your soul - it can be junk food all day or a balanced diet. Be more selective about what you allow into your psyche - garbage in, garbage out.

I listen to audiobooks constantly, on a variety of topics. I listen while I'm driving, before I go to sleep and whenever I possibly can. Sometimes books on mindset, sometimes business, sometimes mysteries of the mind, world and the universe, sometimes fiction, and sometimes something else entirely. I'm absorbing new and different information, expanding my vocabulary along the way, and getting the synapses in my mind firing. The more you expand your mind in a positive way, the more room it has for positivity, and the vaster your mental vision becomes.

Life is more, much more, than what's directly in front of you. By seeking out knowledge, superfood for your mind, and expanding your perspective, you will see that clearly. The good news is that you can do this part without even leaving your room.

14

What is power?

So, here we are. Me and you. You and me. We've taken this brief journey together - a small, but important piece of a long and fulfilling journey called life. Will you have setbacks? Absolutely. But you will have those setbacks whether or not you're living your most empowered life.

I can't thank you enough for investing your time with me and I could only be more grateful, if and only if, this pamphlet has opened your mind and helped to put you on the path to your yet to be unlocked power.

That said, at last, I should give you a little more on what I believe to be this thing we call power.

First, what is *not* power? Power is not holding something over someone's head or threatening them to have control over them. Power is certainly not forcing anyone to do anything against their will. That is known as extortion.

If you are starting a business, do you have to figure out a way to get people on a path and actually pay them? Unless you are all getting paid in sweat equity, yes, you have to pay them. But pay is not the reason they will want to work with you or stay with you. There are many places to work and get a paycheck. If they don't like you or your culture, they will leave or worse, they will stay, and the last thing you want is anyone that feels forced to work with you even though they hate every minute of it. If you want to be a boss, or a leader, or in "power", check your ego at the door. Your power comes from them which means you work for them. In turn, they work hard for you.

Some say power is the acquisition of knowledge and I agree. Some say the application of knowledge, in other words, learning and applying or taking action, on what you've learned - and I agree. Some say self control, meaning control over your thoughts and subsequently control over your actions - and I agree. Discipline, kindness, thoughtfulness, drive, empowerment of others - agree, agree, agree, agree and agree.

You want power? Go give someone a genuine compliment and observe what happens. Watch their guard drop and defenses turn to bashfulness. Pay attention to the appearance of happiness whether through their smile or the glimmer that flashes through the eyes.

Some would say happiness is power AKA peace of mind, a mindset, inner freedom and you guessed it, I would have to agree.

Definiteness of purpose - power.

Properly utilizing your greatest asset which is your time - power.

Taking the high road every time - power.

A vision of you harnessing your power:

It took me a little while to learn me, and what I really wanted. I had to go deep within. My only regret is a regret shared by most people who've unlocked their inner power - I only regret I didn't start on my path sooner. So here's your chance to get started now.

Close your eyes tight and think about who you want to become. What does this *you* look like? How much money do they make? Where does this you vacation? Do they help other people? If so, how? Professionally, charitably, as a mentor? All of the above. What do they do for fun?

Last question, is this version of you actually possible to manifest? In other words, can you actually get there?

Yes.

That is the answer.

Is it worth the consistent mindset training and the daily work that it will take to get there?

Yes.

Are you willing to commit to doing it? This last question is the most important one and not for the obvious reason - at least to me. It's most important not because of your answer, it's because of the question itself.

Folded inside the question, is the implication that this, all of it, all that you want to be and more, is a choice. You decide.

The thing that scares you about answering yes to the question - are you willing to commit to doing the work - is not whether or not you believe that you can get there by doing the work, it's the actual work or just the commitment or both.

It's a little scary when you have that aha moment and realize, yes, this is within my reach and it's up to *me* to reach my arms out past my fear, past all my doubts and insecurities, and grab it. What's worse is when you realize it's up to you and you alone.

There is no one to blame if you don't get there, but you are to blame if you don't try. The good news is that a serious and resolute commitment and trying day in and day out, means you are using your power within. If you commit and you truly try and don't fully get there because maybe you just don't live long enough to make it all come true - well, to me, you discovered your power and you died a success.

If you resolve to get there and become that best version of you and you *do* get there, great! But please be careful. It's easy to forget the old struggle, and to forget about that commitment and what it took to train yourself and your mindset. In other words, don't let your guard down. This is a time when you feel fantastic, and you should - you're on top of the world, but continue to be disciplined.

The word revert exists for a reason. It means to *return to a previous state*. The same way you mentally prepared and trained your mind to unlock your power to get you to your personal mountaintop, is the way you need to train your mind by reaffirming and reminding yourself and staying disciplined, to keep you on top of your personal mountaintop.

And if you slip a little, it's okay. You're human. Dust yourself off and get back on track.

May your continued discipline and awareness of your thoughts and your mind, and awareness of your inner animal's innocent desire to suddenly chase after something that's bad for you, like a bright yellow tennis ball bouncing into the expressway, be your grappling hooks that help you cling to that summit.

Power takes on several forms, but I believe those forms are all interconnected to some degree. Power does not come from the stars aligning. Power comes from within. Once you realize that your true power is in you and always has been, when you look up, you will realize the stars have been aligned the whole time.

THE END OF THIS PAMPHLET

THE TURNING POINT IN YOUR STORY

www.ingramcontent.com/pod-product-compliance
Lightning Source LLC
Chambersburg PA
CBHW030915080526
44589CB00010B/315